STOP INVESTING IN BULLSHIT

BE SMART, TURN THE TABLES
_____

TABLE OF CONTENTS

CLOTHES 5
CARS 7
UNNECESSARY INSURANCE PAYMENTS 9
REDESIGNING HOMES 10
RECREATIONAL DRUGS 12
STRIP CLUB 14
DRINKING 16
SHOES 18
SMARTPHONES AND OTHER DEVICES 20

It is my personal experience that most people have a rather superficial understanding of what investing requires. In practice, I have seen people make costly mistakes with lasting financial implications. For a proper understanding of this seemingly simple yet intricate term, we must first deconstruct the meaning of the word itself. Investment is the process of allocating money to generate profit and returns. Investing simply means putting money and resources forward in hopes of gaining higher value in the future. It is quite unfortunate that people are still unable to make a clear distinction between investment and wasteful spending. By far the most compelling reason why people struggle with investing is because of the addictive consumer culture that is commonplace today. When it comes to spending on the wrong things there is no denying that it doesn't matter what nationality, race, or communities you come from, you are most likely to get caught up with trying to keep up with the "Joneses"! However, reckless spending is becoming widespread. What I am desperately trying to communicate here is that investment is not just an action but a lifestyle!

Let's face the fact! Spending money on the things you like is an enjoyable and rewarding experience.

Jewelry, a new car, clothes, shoe's and other beautiful things serve to increase our pleasures and greatly improve our human experience. It is worth mentioning though that these pleasures are more often than not short-lived. It is truly a dilemma and here's why. We live in the moment and the finer things of life serve to amplify the excitement and pleasures of those moments. However, getting the finer things of life at the expense of making real investments puts our entire financial future in jeopardy and at the risk of failure. In contrast, having investments would provide a sense of security and self-worth. But it comes at the cost of sacrificing your moments. Some might argue that this is an easy choice to make. Yet when the rubber meets the road, it is undoubtedly a daunting challenge for many.

But what if I told you, you could have it all! What if I told you that you could make investments while enjoying the finer things of life? It sounds farfetched and rightfully so. However, for the few that have mastered the art of playing this game, the art of investing can easily be a win-win situation.

Some schools of thought would argue that investment only comes through the painful sacrifice of forgoing every momentary pleasure. While this is a truth and a necessity in some cases, I am here to preach a different yet effective approach. It should be asserted that investment is a lifestyle and not mere action. Some people have cultivated the regrettable lifestyle of investing in BULLSHIT! To those that fall in this category, there is a better way which I would reveal shortly. Humans, like many other creatures on the face of the earth, tend to perpetuate habits.

Many people are hooked on the habit of investing in things that only bring momentary gratification (A.K.A investing in BS!). To those in this category, I say STOP investing in BULLSHIT! If you fall on the other end of the investment spectrum, those who have chosen to tow the path of painfully and grudgingly investing, I strongly recommend that you listen closely to what I'm about to share. Investment can be a win-win for everyone.

There is a need to clarify the difference between wasteful spending and spending on things you like. What is wasteful spending? This is when your spending is often based on emotional impulses with no benefit whatsoever either in the short term or in the long run. A fine example of wasteful spending is seeing a gym membership ad and paying for it without ever going. On the other hand, spending on the things you like means that you use your money to get the things that give you gratification and value even if it's for the short term.

Incurring unnecessary expenses through wasteful spending typically is a behavioral problem that might require therapy to fix. However, spending on the things you care about can be spun around to also be a beneficial and profitable investment at the same time.

You have been taught that you are either an investor or a consumer. Traditional investing like Warren Buffet will be drudgery for most people in our day and age. Also, there are millions of things out there trying to get you to spend your money on bs. The trick is to be both an investor and a consumer. Here is how you straddle the line to get the best of both worlds.

CLOTHES

Clothes and fashion, in general, are loved by many around the world. It is not unusual to find that people spend a lot of resources on clothes and for good reasons. Everyone loves the thrill of shopping. Clothes and fashion offer the unique opportunity to reinvent one's image and appearance. Many perks come with shopping and having new clothes. Aside from the excitement, it can be very therapeutic. Everyone loves to look good and wear things that are in vogue. Even when you become addicted to having the latest clothes and jewelry on the shelf, it does not feel wrong because it is particularly rewarding.

Unfortunately, if you have a knack for shopping and buying new clothes, you are certainly not making any investments. You are simply spending on your immediate short-term gratification. If you are addicted to having the latest fashion and collections of clothes, shoes, and jewelry, there is a good chance that this would cause serious damage to your financial stability.

Traditionally, you had two options. The first option which I would refer to fondly as the "Warren Buffets" approach is to forgo your passion for having nice clothes and focus entirely on investments. The second approach is to continue along the path of your passion and find yourself in a financial mess. However, there is a third approach that I have implemented successfully. I simply started a clothing line!

CLOTHES

Starting a clothing line meant that I would enjoy my passion for shopping while making money in the process. Instead of being a mere consumer, I have created a situation where I can enjoy my proclivity while making worthwhile investments at the same time. Start an online retail store, start a cloth review channel, or start flipping clothes on eBay. The bottom line is to get involved in the business of it!

CARS

It is common knowledge that cars are a liability. But we can all agree that cars are some of the most pleasurable things in life. If you happen to be a car enthusiast, no one can blame you for that. For the car enthusiast, cars are more than a means of transportation and comfort. It is a demonstration of status, style, fashion, and class. You have to get the latest brands. When it comes to having a passion for cars, the risk of going bankrupt is much higher. It is a very expensive habit. So, here is Chad. He is a Nurse anesthetist and earns somewhere between $180,000 to $200,000 annually. His income is quite decent enough to maintain a superb lifestyle and to make tangible investments. He is quite prudent with his earnings but he has a habit for cars. Chad happens to like big badass cars. His love for big cars is, in part, an attempt to compensate for his profession. Being a nurse anesthetist is often viewed as a feminine job. However, having a fleet of big cars would not only satisfy his habit but would give him the status and public image he had always desired to create. Chad does not have a problem whipping out his credit card when it comes to buying a hot car. He has a total of three cars and he still feels inclined to make new purchases. He made one-off payments on his first two cars. The third, however, required a payment plan. Chad is in his third car and he is showing no signs of slowing down. There are many Chads out there who just have a flair for cars. The sad reality is that cars are depreciating assets and would have negative consequences on your finances. The trick is to transform your love for cars into a lucrative business. There are several ways you can turn this liability into an investment. You can enlist your car for corporate car services, airport shuttle services, medical services, or car rental services such as "Turo" which is my personal choice. These are effective ways to create income from car ownership. The game is to flip the tables around. Move your positioning from being a mere consumer to making investments and generating income. It's not a bad idea to go into car sales as well. This is particularly relevant if you enjoy using cars for a short while before selling them off for newer purchases.

UNNECESSARY INSURANCE PAYMENTS

It is funny how some people feel the need to have everything insured. Insurance is relevant and has its applications. Nonetheless, getting insurance on any and everything can be disadvantageous to your income and finances. Insurance is one of those things that is both an investment and a liability depending on how you approach it. There is no telling when you are crossing the line with insurance policies. However, some insurance policies sound like a waste of resources. My advice to you is to make sure that you have the main 3 insurance policies, which are health, life, and car! Do your due diligence to research insurances that you need and don't really need before signing away unnecessary money.

REDESIGNING HOMES

While homes can be a valuable asset and a worthwhile investment, the habit of redesigning homes can quickly create serious financial problems. Being passionate about homes is a good thing. However, too much of a good thing can easily be a bad thing. The cost of redesigning a home is quite pricey. However, just like people with a flair for cars, some people have a passion for remodeling their homes and can easily do so three or more times a year. Financial success is a delicate thing that requires being shrewd. Sadly, most people can't get past their habit.

So, Susan inherited a million dollars and a beautiful home, with no mortgage or liability insurance. She hit the jackpot with this one. She decides she is going to live in the house. She has a flair for redesigning homes and regularly engages in this habit. Susan's friends are worried because the house looks different nearly every time they visit. She will install new lights, repaint, add new fittings and fixtures each time. On average she spends as much as $75,000 annually.

Redesigning your home can easily be termed investing in Bullshit when it is done frequently. The reason is that while homes are assets, they may not be investments. In the case of Susan, she invests $75,000 annually with no returns, just the short-term gratification of a new-looking home. If you are like Susan and can't stop redesigning your home, it will be best to turn the tables on the situation.

Investing in BS simply means you are operating on the level of an addicted consumer. The goal is to transform from an addicted consumer to a passionate entrepreneur. Instead of redesigning your home three times a year, you can offer your skill in interior home designing as a professional service. There is a big market for home designers and this can be a major investment.

Starting a blog and Instagram page that showcases what you do with your home is a step in the right direction. This blog can easily show the world how you transform your home space. Instagram is also a powerful platform to attract potential customers. The idea is to flip the table on your habit in a way that makes it constructive and not destructive to your finances. The other option is to rent it out as a high-end seasonal vacation home. Or to put the home on Airbnb. The bottom line is, you have to make your habit work for you!

RECREATIONAL DRUGS

When it comes to financial investments and spending, you have to be real with yourself. If you ever heard the saying "numbers don't lie," best believe it to be true. As I pointed out earlier, humans, like other creatures on the face of the earth, tend to cultivate habits. There is nothing more habit-forming than recreational drugs. Let me make it abundantly clear that I do not in any way shape or form support the use of illegal or harmful drugs. However, I know for a fact that there is a recreational drug that offers immense benefits, called cannabis being a fine example! It is my personal experience that cannabis offers a host of therapeutic benefits to the body and mind. There have been tons of research on its extensive efficacy and therapeutic applications. However, that is beside the point. While some people use cannabis socially, others use it very frequently and habitually. The difference between social and habitual users is in the financial implication for both parties. Interestingly, many habitual users are completely oblivious to how much they spend on cannabis. A person smoking a pack of cigarettes a day spends about $250 a week on cigarettes. That is $250 on bs! Unlike cigarettes, cannabis is more expensive and has therapeutic benefits which make it okay to overindulge. Just like cannabis, many other recreational drugs could have an undesirable impact on your finances when consumed habitually.

So, Anthony is heavy on a bunch of recreational drugs. He enjoys smoking weed for a variety of reasons. It helps him with his anxiety and he enjoys the feel of it. Anthony spends as much as 350 bucks and much more anytime he has company. He knows the varieties of strains and understands the benefits they provide.

I am not going to denigrate in any way, shape, or form the use of recreational drugs. I feel the government hasn't caught on to its immeasurable benefits. However, I am all about the numbers here. The numbers show that Anthony has naively fallen into the circus of investing in bs! Asking Anthony to stop smoking cannabis is never going to happen. Like always, the goal is to turn the table in a way that this habit becomes an investment. Instead of being a habitual consumer, how about starting your cannabis edibles or becoming a legal cannabis grower. We can all agree that the "Warren buffet" approach isn't going to work in this situation. Anthony isn't going to forgo smoking cannabis for nothing. However, he can spin the situation around to give himself a financial advantage. He has to get into the business of it. Whether it is selling edibles or retailing, Anthony has to move away from being a mere consumer and into becoming an investor.

STRIP CLUB

There is no denying the fact that sex sells. Over the centuries, the capitalist society has caught on to this fact and continues to exploit it to the fullest. What we find today is the hyper-sexualization of women and men to monetize sex. Everywhere you go, you are constantly reminded of sex. The reason for this is that capitalist society wants your money. It is everywhere! It is in the television commercials, it is on the billboards, it is on social media and everywhere you turn your head to look. It is nearly impossible to keep sex off your mind in our day and age. One would think that only romantic movies should have connotations of sex. It is nearly impossible to see a comedy film these days without sexual suggestion. It's everywhere! These days most comedians cannot deliver full material without sexual suggestions. It makes people laugh, it makes people cry, it makes people excited and it stays on the top of our minds. The commercialization of sex is a good thing and a bad thing. However, I am not here to talk about the moralistic implications of sex. To be completely honest, I feel like it is the times we live in and you just have to adapt. My concern is entirely focused on how you can win financially in this climate.

While strip clubs are traditionally a male thing, women are increasingly becoming hooked on the strip club culture, and for good reason. I am not here to denigrate going to the strip clubs. It is a pleasurable experience filled with

STRIP CLUB

provocative excitement. Some might argue that it is therapeutic and helps the body and mind relax from the hustle and bustle of our daily lives. By all means, do what makes you happy so long as you are winning financially.

You'd be amazed at how much strippers make each night. While strippers' income is influenced by a variety of factors, I will have you know they are some of the most well-paid people in society and their earnings are fully sponsored by your habit.

Jackson owns a thriving mechanic shop and an impressive clientele that caters exclusively to celebrities. He has a fantastic team of workers and generates a whopping $100,000 in monthly earnings. He is a big earner and spends generously on his habits. Jackson spends as much as $5000 weekly on average at strip clubs. You might argue that Jackson spends way too much in the strip club but you'd be amazed to find people spend much more than that. At this point, Jackson is just a mere addicted consumer. Even for a celebrity mechanic, this habit will prove fatal and potentially dangerous to his finances. Just as the popular saying goes with men and sex, Jackson would keep looking for better experiences and this will dig deeper and deeper into his finances.

Let's take a step away from Jackson and explore my personal experience. If I calculate how much money I have spent on bottles, strippers by the name of "Diamond" lol, and VIP sections, it's mind-blowing. It could easily be as much as a million bucks and I'm being so serious right now! There is nothing wrong with the club scene. My favorite club is a strip club lol.

After a while, I realized that all the years, I wasted my money and can't get it back. I started to investigate the financial implications of my habit. I was shocked by my findings and decided to turn the tables.

I did my research on how to invest into running and owning my own club whether it's a bar, lounge, strip club, etc. So now that you know what my favorite type of club is, you must know and believe that one day I will be running and owning my own. REMEMBER SEX SELLS! And that will be investing in myself. The goal is to turn the tables on your habit. Move from a mere consumer to an investor. Jackson would have to figure out how to benefit. He could seek investments from his clientele in a joint business. The ultimate goal is to win with your habits

DRINKING

Excessive drinking is certainly indicative of a problem and might require counseling and some sorts of intervention. However, for those with a responsible knack for strong beverages, drinking can still be an expensive habit with serious financial implications. Alcohol is pleasurable when consumed alone and remains the most important ingredient for exhilarating social gatherings. Everyone enjoys having a drink or two. Drinking is an integral part of adult life and when consumed responsibly, punctuates our experiences with even more gratifying moments. Some people are social drinkers. If you fall in this category then this is certainly not for you. However, for those that have their lifestyle built around drinking, it would be sensible to convert your habit into a profitable venture.

In 2020 the global beer market reached a whopping value of US $623.2 billion, now imagine what it is now! This goes to show that it is a very big industry and that a lot of people drink frequently.

How you get your drink is another factor that must be considered. For those that go to bars, the cost of drinking is significantly higher. If you get two drinks twice a week, the estimated expenses will range from $150 to $250 a month. Interestingly, there are levels to drinking and this makes it all the more dangerous to overindulge. Alcohol comes in a robust variety that includes wine, beer, vodka, whiskey, brandy, cognac, and much more. Depending on the brand and quality, these beverages can come with a hefty price tag. Just as with every other habit you enjoy, drinking grows commensurately to earning power. This simply means that people prefer drinking the finer stuff when they can afford it. With all these considerations in mind, it becomes easy to see how a habit of alcohol could have undesirable financial consequences.

Investors see money very differently than the average joe. The goal is to cultivate a mind for investment. For the average income earner, spending as much as 500 bucks on alcohol monthly translates to spending on bs! It is my personal experience that drinking is a way of life for those that enjoy it. I can't tell you how many times I've considered stopping for health concerns. Thankfully, I haven't had any complications from drinking. I am not asking you to stop drinking the finer stuff or to stop enjoying your beverage. But if you have a knack for drinking and spend as much as 500 bucks a month, you should consider flipping the tables by investing in your habit.

Some will argue that there are no ways to get involved in a business. To those, I reply by saying that there is always a way. I'm in the process of developing my own brand of wine because that is what I enjoy drinking, especially when I'm writing. There are several ways to invest in yourself when it comes to alcohol.

It is a reasonable argument to say that creating your beverage requires a strong financial backbone. While this is true, you can always get involved in other aspects of the business. You must look at the business model of the business and see where you can fit in. While I intend to go all the way to the top as a manufacturer, you can achieve this as a retailer or distributor or by owning a bar or in some other capacity. The goal is to get involved.

SHOES

To the shoe lover, shoes are a big deal! There is no denying the socio-cultural importance of shoes in American society and particularly amongst minorities. Fashion has shifted the relevance of shoes significantly from just being a mere footgear for protection and mobility. Take sneakers for example, from being a mere sports gear for athletes, it became ingrained in hip-hop culture and soon morphed into the single most important fashion statement for men. The sneakers appeal strongly to minority teenage and college men by offering the opportunity to create their style. Whether it's sneakers or other kinds of shoes, the shoe enthusiast will show no sign of slowing down. It is not uncommon to find people anticipating the release of new sneakers and rushing to stores to get them. This is regardless of whether or not they need it. Buying shoes becomes spending on bs when you have several good pairs at home and still feel the need to get a new one. You'd be amazed to find the number and scale of a struggling college student's sneaker collection.

I won't sit here and judge your proclivities and appetites. However, I would warn you about the financial costs of your actions and remind you of the need to stop investing in bs. You cannot remain a mere consumer. You have to get your head in the money-making game. Global sneakers market revenue was valued at approximately 70 billion. You can't be caught sleeping on this one.

You have to wake up and actively pursue a piece of the pie. Going by the above-mentioned stats, it is a very big pie indeed.

I'm not the biggest shoe person, I usually just buy shoes as needed. I have associates that probably have every Jordan shoe ever made, and there is nothing wrong with that but let me give you some tips on how you can invest in yourself.

If you are a shoe enthusiast there are several ways you can start investing. Like I pointed out earlier, you don't necessarily have to start at the top of the value chain. The reason is that investing at the top of the chain often requires a lot of money. For those with resources and means, it is not a bad idea to design your shoe line and get people to buy your shoes. This is the top of the game when it comes to investing in shoes. Investing at this level will commensurately translate into making a lot of profit. Understanding the nuances of the shoe line industry is important. Getting a team of designers and professionals will be a step in the right direction. In the world of investment, if you sow big, you reap even bigger.

For the middle class or struggling college student, investing in a shoe line might be out of reach, however, there are several other investment opportunities in the value chain. You can get into the shoe reselling industry otherwise known as the shoe flipping industry. You'd be amazed by how much you can generate from flipping shoes. This is a worthwhile investment but requires a little bit of entrepreneurial input. Nonetheless, flipping shoes offers a superb opportunity for investment and profit. I know for a fact that people make as much as $500 or more a day from flipping shoes. Being a shoe collector and retailer is a fantastic way to invest. When it comes to the shoe business, the opportunities are limitless. How about selling used shoes online? The only requirement is to create a platform where people can sell quality used shoes to you online which would, in turn, be sold to others online. This might require inspection for quality assurance but it would certainly catch on in no time.

SMARTPHONES AND OTHER DEVICES

The craze for smartphones and other electronic devices is at a timely high and it is only going to get more intense. We have 5G technology now and this is guaranteed to stimulate an unprecedented rush from the consumer market. Smartphones and electronic devices are usually functional products that provide certain services to users. However, like most valuable items, smartphones, and electronic devices have become a symbol of status, class, and sophistication. It can be argued that people spend a lot of money on smartphones and devices to keep up with the latest trends in technology. However, this claim cannot be further from the truth. What we have seen is a mania for smartphones and other electronic devices in a way that is driven by fad. If you have a weakness for phones and other devices, you are certainly not alone. There are millions of people out there with your passion or should I say craze? Everyone wants to use the latest phone and devices. Interestingly, these devices are far more often than not, underutilized.

SMART PHONES AND OTHER DEVICES

Understanding your habits is very important if you want to navigate the world of investments unscathed. "Know thyself!" If you buy every new iPhone and wait for new releases, you have a serious problem in that regard. I don't want to explore the cost implications of being addicted to purchasing phones and electronic devices. I'd rather explore ways in which you can flip the table and stop inviting in bs.

Your appetite for various consumer goods can be a hindrance to worthwhile investments. However, there are also challenges associated with social pressure which many people are susceptible to. It is a common perception to assume that only teenagers bow to peer pressure and influences. While this holds some merit, it is not entirely true. You'd be amazed by the extent to which adults try to conform to societal expectations. It's one scenario to engage in profligate spending because of your own appetite, it's a whole different scenario to spend lavishly because of pressure from the media and society. Social media has taken pressure to a whole new stratosphere. More than ever before, people are inclined to compare their lifestyle with others. The reason why this scenario is particularly problematic is that your finances have been hijacked by advertisers, peer groups and social media. At this point, you are NOT spending based on your needs and interests. More than ever before, people are driven by the fear of missing out on new products and the need to impress. This problem typically manifests in the way of spending on luxurious and overpriced goods. I can't tell you how many times I've seen people buy high-end luxury cars just to keep up with the joneses. Do you really need a Mercedes or would you be just fine driving a Toyota Camry? Are you buying things to please people and to fit in? This pattern is a never-ending cycle that would inevitably cause serious injury to your finances. There is no middle ground! Investment translates into financial growth while profligacy is tantamount to financial suicide. The need to impress could easily create a downward spiral that leads to untold financial difficulties. As an investor, you must turn a blind eye to social pressure and the need to conform.

Investing is the willingness to see the bigger picture. Don't be deceived! It is nearly impossible to invest without sacrifice. It does not necessarily have to be in extremes like Warren Buffett's approach, but you will have to sacrifice regardless. For smartphone, gadget, and electronic lovers, the key is to look at the value chain and identify where you can fit in. The smartphone is not showing any signs of slowing for no one. If you have a flair for mobile devices, it would be wise to discover ways to invest and profit from this proclivity. You could add accessories to phones, open a phone and mobile device shop, or simply buy shares in startups. Whatever you do, don't sit idly as a mere consumer.

Several personality traits must be cultivated to become a good investor. Being able to forecast is particularly important. One other relevant criterion is diversifying your portfolio. I can't tell you how many investments I have going. I'm still looking for new investment opportunities to be involved in. Changing your proclivities and habits can be difficult for some and nearly impossible for others. Lead your habits and emotions in contrast to letting your habits and emotions lead you. As an investor, you have to take control of your habits and behavior.

If you are passionate about something, don't engage with it in a way that makes you lose money. Be passionate about it in a way that makes you earn instead. We live in a capitalist world. Being a mere consumer will only create a life with no real tangible investments or financial security.

Identify your habits with the primary aim of investing profitably in them. Don't let your habits lead you down the path of wasteful spending. Understanding the nature of your habits and ways to invest profitably is the key. People tend to find material success when they positively pursue their habits.

IN CLOSING

Let's focus on being more of an investor than a consumer, it will be beneficial to you and your family in the long run. So if you fit the description of any of the characters in this book take a step back and explore ways to turn the tables by becoming an investor. Thank you for taking the time to read my book and I wish you the best endeavors on your journey to becoming the best investor I know you can be!

COACHRAY

www.ingramcontent.com/pod-product-compliance
Lightning Source LLC
Chambersburg PA
CBHW070322220526
45465CB00013B/2204